COLLECTING
WOODEN NICKELS

COLLECTING WOODEN NICKELS

*A Journey of Stepping Out On Faith
and Receiving Everything Life Brings*

Katrina Mosley Stinnett

COLLECTING WOODEN NICKELS

Published by Purposely Created Publishing Group™
Copyright © 2019 Katrina Mosley Stinnett
All rights reserved.

No part of this book may be reproduced, distributed or transmitted in any form by any means, graphic, electronic, or mechanical, including photocopy, recording, taping, or by any information storage or retrieval system, without permission in writing from the publisher, except in the case of reprints in the context of reviews, quotes, or references.

Author Photo of Katrina Mosley Stinnett taken by Lasting Look Photography, Owners: Larry Mosley Jr. and Charletha Patrick Mosley; Mobile, Alabama; Facebook: @LarryMosleyJr

Printed in the United States of America

ISBN: 978-1-64484-098-6

Special discounts are available on bulk quantity purchases by book clubs, associations and special interest groups.
For details email: sales@publishyourgift.com
or call (888) 949-6228.

For information log on to www.PublishYourGift.com

This book is dedicated to:

The Achievers. My Readers.

Also… my parents, Larry and Rose Ann Mosley; my husband, Quentin; my brother and sister-in law, Larry and Charletha Mosley; my nieces, London Yvonne and Laylah Rose; my mother-in-law and father-in-law, Robert and Donna Fay Hammonds; and my Jack Russell puppy dog, Major.

Thank you all for supporting my vision.

Table of Contents

Check on the Strong ix

Introduction 1

Conversation 1: *The First Wooden Nickel* 9

Conversation 2: *A Way Out* 21

Conversation 3: *What's Weight Got to Do With It* 39

Conversation 4: *The Good Job* 49

Conversation 5: *The Hated Promotion* 59

Conversation 6: *Let the Games Begin* 67

Conversation 7: *The Change Up* 77

Conversation 8: *No More Growth* 91

Conversation 9: *Forgiving Wooden Nickels* 99

Conversation 10: *Time to Step Out and Receive Everything Life Brings* 107

Acknowledgments 119

Time to Soar! 123

About the Author 127

Check on the Strong

Check on the one who wants to work all day & night long.

Check on the one that is smiling but can't seem to get along.

CHECK ON THE STRONG.

Check on the one you keep hearing say, "I'm always wrong."

Check on the one who is always singing the same song.

CHECK ON THE STRONG.

Check on the one who feels they don't belong.

Check on the one you keep telling to be strong.

CHECK ON THE STRONG.

Introduction

GOD created everyone with a purpose and everything GOD plans will come to pass. Sophia Jameson believed that she was living proof that GOD did in fact place a special gift inside of everyone. Sophia believed we are all able to do any and everything in life if we have the right mindset. Sophia had to stop looking at the presence of storms as the absence of GOD.

She had a normal life. She and her friend, Camille Holloway, even joined the Air Force together after high school. Sophia had the hope of serving a few years and coming home to start a business. While in the military, she finally had the opportunity to see some of the world and more importantly the places she had read about when she was young. She got married and divorced within a three year span, then she finally settled down with a new husband. Things were starting to seem like they were turning around. She even landed a good job. But Sophia's life was still filled with ups and downs. Over time, she saw some of her friends come and go. But her friends Eva, Camille, Candace, and Kellie, from her small hometown of Sewadville, had been there, at least for the things she wanted to share with them. Sophia has seen numerous loved ones pass away, witnessed things that no one should ever see, and experienced things that up until now she was afraid and ashamed to share with her friends. But, all of that changed at their latest Drinks and Conversations Dinner where Sophia and her friends enjoyed deep discussions about childhood and relationship drama, sexism, racism, and discrimination in the workplace.

The depth of the conversations between Sophia and her friends go hand in hand with what they drink. They have held conversations while drinking water, those are light in subject. And those held when drinking wine are deep conversations.

Travelling across the globe opened Sophia's eyes wide to the many things going on in the world. That was the driving force behind her wanting to develop the Drinks and Conversations Dinner. It was a way for Sophia and her friends to vent to one another and have fun being together at the same time.

During dinner, she breaks down to her friends the types of people she has seen during her travels. Sophia came to realize there are three types of people in this world… The Doubters, The Dreamers, and The Achievers. Sophia had been The Dreamer for so long and had been allowing The Doubter to influence her, but no more! Sophia decided she would become The Achiever, no matter what.

By Sophia's observation, The Doubters are the people sitting back talking about the things they want to do, the ideas they have, and the places they want to go, but they aren't doing anything to make it happen because they are always doubting themselves or others. The Doubters are also the same people talking about other people and they love drama.

Then you have The Dreamers. They are always dreaming or thinking about doing something, but they do not get any further than just having the dream because they let the influence of others get in the way. Basically, The Dreamer allows The Doubter to get in their head and discourage them from becoming an Achiever.

Lastly, the people who follow through are The Achievers. These people set goals and let nothing stop them from reaching their goals. The best part about The Achiever is that while they are working to finish one goal, they are setting the next goal. Being an Achiever does not mean they are the most educated, although they can be, but what stands out about them is the fact that they are the most motivated people in the world.

It took a discriminatory act at work for Sophia to take a step back and ask herself how she felt about her life and business.

Before that incident, Sophia spent most of her time as a Dreamer. After that incident, she made the choice to dive into her next step in life as an Achiever and to not stop until her business was successful and able to make a difference, not only in her and her husband's lives but to empower others also. Sophia's ultimate goals are to empower and inspire people to follow their dreams and to look at their businesses and life as Achievers and make it happen.

We all want to overcome the odds and make success happen for our businesses or marriages. Sophia spent a lot of time researching businesses or speaking with people in business, and through their stories of success she realized that these people had the focus and drive to maintain as Achievers not just as Dreamers.

Sophia is no longer afraid to share with the world the many things she has gone through because those experiences, good and bad, have been teaching tools. She feels successful because she is making her dreams a reality with her husband, Christopher, and her friends by her side. They are all passionate about their businesses. They argue and laugh, but they are strategic, hardworking, and devoted to building strong brands.

Sophia and Christopher are quickly learning that anything is possible, and they will see great results as long as they work hard and work together. They went through struggles separately and they have struggled together, but they felt they were in the trenches for long enough and it was time to lift their heads, pull themselves out of those holes, and work hard to bring more balance to their lives.

Throughout this book, you will go on a short journey with Sophia and her friends as they realize they were not only doing what they were told not to do (which was take wooden nickels), but they have been collecting them for years.

The most important thing to do when you realize you are holding on to something that is invaluable is to get rid of it before it takes you down with it. And they have been holding on to a lot of wooden nickels.

You will get to know the stories of small town girls who go from being Dreamers to Achievers and CEOs of their own company. This does not mean your journey will end the same as theirs because what GOD has for you is for you, and what He has for them is for them. Taking risks and facing fears and failures were ways for them to get right, not just in their lives but with GOD.

Please let *Collecting Wooden Nickels* guide and encourage you to stop collecting wooden nickels and empower you to step out on faith to receive everything life brings to you. Let the stories of Sophia and her friends inspire you to be the best at whatever you desire. Let their truths guide you onto a new path of hope. Even if you are down due to losing your job and you think your career is over, the only thing that can hold you back is you. You are your own worst enemy. One thing you must remember is that it only takes one raindrop to raise the sea, so be that one raindrop. Make the changes you desire in your life and don't take wooden nickels!

Before we get started on your journey, what is your choice of drink when holding a conversation with your friends?

_____

_____

Use the lines at the end of each conversation to think about your wooden nickels and join in on the discussion at the closed group ***Drinks and Conversations*** on social media.

Conversation

1

The First Wooden Nickel

Sophia Jameson prepared for another Drinks and Conversations Dinner with her friends and family. Their monthly meeting had grown and was starting to bring friends and families closer. These ladies always had a way of making sure Sophia's light stayed bright no matter how many times she tried to cut it off.

Eva Davis arrived early, as she always did, to help prepare food or spend some alone time with Sophia. The pair were sitting in the living room having a drink while dinner was in the oven.

Eva said to Sophia, "I believe when people think of you, they think: personal strength, business empowerment, and social contributor. Look at your house right now. You have your business stuff everywhere, but it's organized. You stay on top of things and I don't know how in the world you do it."

Sophia and Eva were also waiting for a few more ladies, including their other best friend Camille Holloway, who was typically late for everything. Camille was the life of any party. And when these ladies got together, it was always a great time. They were best friends working regular jobs while secretly building their own empires. Sophia worked as a project manager for seven years after retiring from military service and was in the process of purchasing an event center. Eva worked as a paralegal at a large law firm for the past ten years and she was a cake baker and decorator. Camille worked as the manager of a department in a retail clothing store for eight years and was also a hair stylist who had recently retired from military service too. All of them had hopes of turning their side businesses into their full-time jobs, but it was happening sooner than any of them thought.

Sophia looked at Eva and said one sentence, "Don't take wooden nickels!"

At that moment, the doorbell rang.

Sophia got up to go to the door while saying, "That's probably Camille."

Sophia opened the door to see her sister, Kellie, and Camille. Kellie was actually Sophia's cousin, but her parents adopted her which made her Sophia's sister too. Kellie used to get into a lot of trouble and was on and off drugs for years. But now she had been spending her time trying to change her life, and of course she was always welcome in Sophia's home.

Sophia said to them, "You two are late as usual. You were about to miss a good conversation."

"Well, I'm here now so let's get it started. I know you two are not just drinking wine coolers," Camille responded, referring to the wine cooler Sophia had in her hand. "Where are the real drinks?" she asked.

They laughed and hugged and headed toward the living room to Eva.

Camille came in the room yelling, "Eva, you are looking good girl!" All four of them laughed while Camille and Kellie hugged Eva.

Camille said, "I'll start with this for now," as her and Kellie grabbed wine coolers and joined Eva and Sophia in the living room. Then she asked, "What are we talking about?"

Sophia responded, "Well, Eva and I were not really talking about anything yet."

Eva chimed in, "Sophia, what do you mean we were not talking about anything when you just said to me, 'Don't take wooden nickels!'"

Camille said, "You mean that thing your grandmother said to us a million times when we were young?"

Kellie responded, "Grandma did say that a lot."

"Yes, exactly that!" Sophia said.

That phrase was embedded inside of all of them at a young age. Sophia had been carrying the phrase with her throughout her life.

Camille said, "Yes. It seemed like it was your grandma's favorite thing to say to us. And you saying that came out of nowhere, but it does seem like a good thought right about now."

"You know, I have been taking and collecting a lot of wooden nickels throughout my life," Sophia said.

Eva responded, "Tell me about it."

Camille said, "I know what you mean right about now."

"Yes, me too!" Kellie said.

Sophia, Eva, and Camille had been best friends since they were children because they all lived in the little country town of Sewadville. Kellie was the same age as Candace, Camille's sister.

Sophia began to tell them stories like none other. Stories of the things she had experienced, and even some things she had never shared with them.

She said, "Let me tell you all about these wooden nickels I have collected over the years. Some of them are good and some of this might be sad, but it's how I got to this place of understanding. It's why I push us so hard to get our businesses off the ground. And as much as I hate to admit it, all of these things that happened to me… they happened to me for a reason. Because of what I'm going through right now on my job, I have really been thinking about all the things I accepted throughout my life. Let me tell you a few things and why I said don't take wooden nickels."

She continued, "I know you all remember Carl."

Eva replied, "Yes, your cousin Nita's brother. Yes, I remember him."

Sophia asked, "Do you remember how he used to always say slick stuff to us and would always talk about sex around us? When we were thirteen years old, he tried to mess around with me."

Eva said, "Me too, that's why I don't like him. And he was old as hell and was trying to get with young girls."

Sophia responded, "Right. And I don't understand why older men see a younger girl as a target. It's funny how they want to do stuff to young girls, but then have the nerve to get mad when someone does or says something out of the way to their daughters. Even though I was scared to say anything to my parents, I immediately told them when it happened. Some of my uncles showed up and were shooting towards Carl and Nita's house in the hope of hitting him because of what he had done. The only person that could calm everybody down was Grandma."

Sophia continued, "My grades went down and I started a downward spiral of bad behavior. I went to therapy because I kept reliving the situation. At that age, I thought that if he said he was sorry, I was going to be all better and everybody would stop being mad about it and everything could go back to how life was before the situation. I didn't get an apology until he was in town and someone robbed him and beat him up and he almost died. I'm still mad at him about it and the situation messed me up for a long time. He is family and was trying to mess with me. I hated him for a long time. I did not want any male to touch me at all. I couldn't even hug my dad for a long time because I was filled with fear. And you know we are from this small country town, so my grandma just made the rule that wherever I was, he couldn't be. Basically, if I was at her house, he couldn't be at her house at the same time. When I showed up to a family function, he needed to leave no matter what because it was Grandma's Law. It was crazy because you know how close I am with Nita. Everyone in the family knew that something happened to me, but they kept it from her. She asked about the situation one day because she kept hearing rumors. She pretty much saw him as her everything, so I told her, 'Yes, something happened to me, and it was a family member.' I left it at that."

Sophia said to the ladies, "I have been through some things and it's crazy because we have never had this discussion. I must tell you this because I have never told you. When we were seventeen, I got pregnant."

Camille said, "What? You were? What happened? Why didn't you tell us?"

Sophia responded, "My mom hit me and called me stupid. She was so mad about the situation. The next morning, she took me down to the clinic and told me I had to have an abortion. I wasn't given a choice in the matter. You know how quiet and naïve I was back then. And, of course, I had nowhere to go, so I did it. My mom was all about protecting the image because she felt like her sister had already ruined it with her drug abuse and Kellie was going down the same path as her mom at the time. Of course, she did not want anyone to know. She told me it was just mass and the baby had not started to form, but I was 11 weeks pregnant. I know now that at 11 weeks the baby had in fact started to form, and I hate myself every day for doing it."

Eva asked, "Wait, Sophia, did this have anything to do with why you had such a hard time getting pregnant or why you kept having miscarriages?"

Sophia replied, "Honestly, Eva, I believe it was the reason. I felt as if I was being punished for killing an innocent child. It is the worst feeling in the world to have to wake up and look at myself in the mirror knowing that no matter how many tests and pokes I go through, I am still unable to carry a child. I went to hell and back throughout my life and I have been sitting back taking it and not saying anything. Just keeping it to myself. And that is why I'm so glad we are having this talk because with what I'm going through right now on my job, I am at a breaking point."

Camille asked, "What did Chris say about the struggles of you two not having a child together?"

Sophia replied, "He is okay with it because he says he only wants to make sure I'm healthy. He does not want me to risk my life to have a child. I get so mad at him because, of course, he already has a boy and a girl with his ex-wife, Natalie. It is just not the same. I mean, I love them as if they were mine, but I am constantly reminded that they are not because when my birthday's or Christmas comes around, I don't even get a card from either one of them. But when the shoe is on the other foot, they are always looking for gifts or wanting some money. I am hoping we will be given the opportunity to at least raise a child. Once everything is finalized with the adoption of the baby girl, we are naming her Sienna Alexandria."

Sophia continued, "Truth be told, there is so much I have been going through and keeping from you all."

Eva responded, "Girl, I am the same way."

Camille and Kellie both chimed in saying, "Me too."

"Well, let's finally talk about it all," Sophia said.

DRINK:

_____

_____

CONVERSATION:

Think back to the first time you can remember when something happened to you or someone did something to you. Did you accept it and allow it to continue, or did you fight back?

_____

_____

_____

_____

Join the conversation on social media at
Drinks and Conversations.

Conversation 2

A Way Out

Eva said, "Honestly, I had an abortion too when we were seventeen. I just never said anything about it. You all know my parents are so religious and I knew they would lose it. You all know my sister, Erica, was pregnant?"

They all responded saying, "Yes, we remember."

Eva said, "It was about a month after Erica told our parents that she was pregnant that I found out that I was pregnant too. I knew they would either kill me, or one of them would have a heart attack. So, I went and did the abortion and never said anything to anyone until today. I never even told Kenny."

Sophia said, "Wow, Girl, we have been through it."

"Sophia, I am okay with it," Eva said, "I do think about it from time to time and wonder about the child, but it was a choice that I made. I just hate that you weren't given a choice and your situation was messed up."

Sophia said, "Let me tell you all, I was so messed up from never getting over the situation with Carl and having to live life with Grandma's Law in effect and other stuff, that after we finished high school, I decided to go into the Air Force because I couldn't deal with things at that time. Camille wasn't ready to leave Sewadville, but she did. Camille and I decided to go into the Air Force together, and she went to the Reserves."

Eva replied, "I never knew that was the reason you two went into the military."

Sophia responded, "Yes, the pregnancy and abortion got in my head along with having to keep the secret from Dwight that I had killed our child. It was hitting me hard. One morning, I woke up and felt like I needed to get away and that was the best way I could make it happen. So I went and picked up Camille, told her what I wanted to do, and she actually said she wanted to go to the recruiting station too because she was thinking about joining the military. We went and joined that same day. It was my way out. My way to escape from the arguments, resentment, guilt, and anger about what I had done and everything that happened."

Camille said, "I really didn't want to go to the military, but when you called, I knew I couldn't let you go alone."

"I never knew that," Sophia said.

"We are friends," Camille responded, "I love you. Plus, I couldn't let you just go through that by yourself."

"Most of my family was supportive," Sophia said, "even when I left for the military, Kellie and my brothers, Thomas and William (Will), were hurt, but I know they understood. Uncle Leon said, 'You are not going to make it. You'll be back in two weeks.' After leaving, I had one goal in mind… to stay longer than two weeks. I didn't have anything to prove to anybody, just myself, but I still wasn't coming back in two weeks.

There were some rough times though, I know you all remember me telling you about the guy that died from the tank rolling over him."

Eva replied, "Yes, I remember that. You were messed up for a long time after that."

Sophia responded, "Yes, I was, but that was nothing compared to going to work and being sexually harassed non-stop. And saying something about it didn't matter because they didn't do anything about it."

Sophia continued, "I know you all remember some of what happened in my first marriage to Jerome, he really put me through hell."

Kellie said, "I remember he was messing around on you, but I don't remember us going into full detail about what happened."

"Sophia, how did you find out about the girlfriend?" Camille asked.

Sophia replied, "I was at our apartment cleaning. We had a big window with a ledge next to the balcony door and he had a number sitting in the window ledge. I looked at the number and it had the name Charlee written on it. I just sat it on the table because it could have been the name of someone in his division. I went on about my business cleaning, but something in me was like, 'Who the hell is Charlee?' I picked up the piece of paper, dialed the number, and a female with an Italian accent answered the phone. I asked was Charlee available and she said, 'Charlotte?' I knew then that he was messing around with this girl. I talked with her for a good while. She told me that he comes to her all the time, he treats her nice, she's pregnant, they are so excited about having a baby, and it's a boy. I was completely calm on the phone and never let Charlotte know that I was pregnant too, also with a baby boy. We ended our call and I lost it.

I was cleaning before the call, but afterward I started to rip up the apartment. I went through everything and found pictures of half-naked women, pictures of him with women, and I even found pictures labeled Charlee and Junior, as well as ultrasound photos. It was apparent he was going to have two Juniors because we had decided to name our son after him too. I was so sick, but this explained everything, especially where he would go when he said he was going on field missions or trainings and would be gone the whole weekend. After all the discoveries for the day, we had a huge argument when he finally got home that evening. That argument ended with him physically assaulting me and leaving me bloody and passed out on the floor.

My friend and neighbor, Naomi, from the apartment across the hall was coming back with groceries and found me on the floor because he had left the front door open. She called an ambulance. When I woke up three days later, I was in the hospital and I was no longer pregnant. I had lost my son due to either stress, the assault, or both. His division moved him out of the house. But the day he came to get his stuff, the military police were with him and he threw my computer printer at me as I was sitting on the couch. I, of course, moved out of the way and the MP's grabbed him and took him out of the apartment with his stuff. Later that night as I showered and washed my hair, I reached for my special detangling solution that I used for easy comb through. You know how curly my hair can get. Well, I realized that he had taken it out of spite, because he was bald and had no use for the stuff.

We had one of those frosty glass windows in the shower and I was so angry at the thought of losing my child, my husband cheating and being verbally and physically abusive, and his girlfriend being pregnant too that I punched the glass while I was in the shower. Naomi came because she heard the sound and was ringing the doorbell like crazy trying to check on me. I got out of the shower and was so numb to any feeling or emotion that I didn't realize that my hands, thighs, and legs were bloody from the shattered glass. I immediately got some towels for the blood and put on some clothes while she called the maintenance people who came and installed a new window. The next day I was supposed to go shopping with my friend, Lanie, but all I had on my mind was that I was done living. I had enough and did not want to deal with another day of sadness and stress. I fell asleep on the couch and woke up because the phone was ringing.

Lanie asked me if we were still going shopping. I really don't remember what I said to her at that moment, but I heard her say, 'I'm coming now' and then she hung up the phone. I had already made up in my mind what I wanted to do; falling asleep on the couch the night before didn't change anything. I disconnected the phone while crying non-stop. As I looked at photos of my family, my ultrasound, me with Jerome, and photos of all of us when we were young, I wondered how my life got to that point. But, it didn't matter because I was ending it and I was doing it before somebody tried to stop me.

I got the sharpest knife from the kitchen that I could find. And just as I was about to cut my wrists, I heard a loud banging at the door and saw that the doorknob was moving because someone was attempting to open the door. The voices on the other side said, 'Sophia, we are here to help you. Your friend, Lanie, asked us to come by and check on you. Can you come open the door for us?' But, the sound of their voices didn't change my mind either. I heard them say, 'We are going to break the door down.' And then I heard Lanie say, 'Sophia, please come open the door. I love you. I need you in my world. Please come open the door.' The sound of Lanie's cracking, crying voice made me stop. Then suddenly I heard the voice of God from within me say, 'Sophia, I have so much planned for you. I need you on Earth for it all to come to pass. Open the door.' God didn't ask me to open the door, He told me to, and I did just that. I put the knife down, got up, and unlocked the door.

They all rushed in. Lanie was hugging me, kissing me, and telling me that she loved me non-stop. They checked me out and told me that I had to go to the hospital. I told them no, I was fine, and that they didn't have to worry about me because I was never going to attempt to do that again. Lanie said she was going to stay with me. Everyone else eventually left. Lanie stayed with me every day for over a month until I left Italy to come back to the United States. I am still friends with Lanie to this day."

Sophia said, "I know you all knew my cousin Diane's daughter, Danika, who passed a few years ago."

Eva and Camille each replied, "Yes, I remember her."

Kellie said, "Of course you know that I know our cousins, Diane and Danika."

"That was sad," Eva said, "because she was in an abusive relationship too and that guy ended up killing her."

Sophia responded, "Yes, I carried that for a while because I felt like I should have said something to my family about what I went through in Italy. I don't know if it would have helped her; I will never know now. But I do regret not saying anything to warn these young girls about the signs of an abusive relationship."

Eva said, "Sophia, maybe that would have happened to her regardless, even with warnings or signs."

"Eva is right, Sophia, because look at my situation," Kellie said. "The things I have gone through have been right there for the world to see."

"So you are completely free now, right?" Camille asked.

Kellie responded, "Yes. As you all know I did kill my husband, Jeffery. I was being abused by him in every way imaginable for years. I called the police so many times, but because he was a cop too, they saw him as an upstanding citizen and they basically did nothing. I started recording him with my phone, taking photos of myself, and emailing them to a secret email account that only I knew about. I would delete the sent emails. I had given instructions to Patricia, at the organization where I volunteer, that if anything ever happened to me to give this information to Sophia and to the police. She wondered also why they wouldn't do anything. I wanted to make sure I was covered and that if something happened to me he would not be able to get away with it. I know I had a rough time when I was younger being on and off drugs and raped by my mom's boyfriends and drug dealers. My mom did not care about me, she only wanted to get her drugs and did not mind selling or exchanging me for them. This pushed me to drugs and to being like her. The child welfare finally allowed me to live at Sophia's house permanently, her parents adopted me. I eventually gave my life to God, got clean, and started getting my life on track. And then, I clearly married the wrong man.

Now that I am out of jail, I do thank God that I was only in there for just over two years, especially since the judge refused to give me bail because his police friends thought Jeff was the greatest police officer and I had just killed him for no reason. Now that I have been cleared of everything, they have been calling trying to apologize. I know it is because of all the evidence I had that proved that he was abusive and that I only killed him in self-defense. My lawyer has filed a case against the judge because of the way I was treated unfairly with no bail and everything. I recently received the letters saying that all of his insurance money, pension, and social security will be coming to me after all because it was self-defense and I was cleared of all charges. We must now wait to see what happens with the lawsuit. I am happy that I finally got a way out and now everyone knows the truth."

"We all have gone through some things. And as Sophia would say, we have been collecting wooden nickels," Camille said.

As Sophia takes the chicken and lasagna out of the oven she replies, "For me, I haven't even scratched the surface because I am dealing with a real issue right now at my job."

"Come on ladies, let's dig in," she continued.

They gather around as Sophia leads them in prayer. Then, they take a look at the spread of roasted chicken, lasagna, salad, assorted fruits, and of course drinks that Sophia has prepared, and they make their plates while sitting at the dinner table continuing their conversation.

Eva says, "You ladies already know some of what I went through with my kids' father, Kenny. Things always had to be his way or no way at all. I remember on the evening of our anniversary, I don't even know which anniversary, because I was still cooking dinner when he came home, he yelled, punched me in my face, cursed at me, opened the back door, and pushed me out. Then, he locked me out of the house. I didn't have my car keys, my phone, or anything. I slept in the garage. I didn't even eat that night. He kept saying that I had to learn because I was supposed to have his dinner ready when he came home. But hell, I was working just like he was. The kids didn't even know about this because they both were staying the night at their friend's houses since it was our anniversary. The next morning before he left, he did unlock the back door, but he didn't tell me."

Sophia said, "Eva, I never knew that. Why didn't you call me? You and the kids could have come to stay over here."

"Sophia, I was embarrassed," Eva responded. "I didn't want anyone to know that Kenny was treating me that way. Kenny and I were the prom king and queen in high school, the star football player and the head cheerleader. So, of course, I wanted the so-called fairytale life to work out. Plus, I wanted to believe Kenny was going to change so I stayed with him. I was still working at the grocery store at the time, waiting for construction to finish for the law office to open, and I wasn't making enough money to take care of myself and the kids too, so I felt like I had to stay."

Sophia, Eva, Camille, and Kellie were all in tears while hugging one another and trying to eat at the same time.

Kellie asked Eva, "What was the thing that made you say enough is enough?"

Eva looked at Kellie with tears in her eyes and said, "It was when my oldest daughter, Jasmine, said to me, 'Mama, it's time for us to leave him. You don't have to take this from him.' Then she said, 'Mama, my friend, Tameka, said he is messing around with her Aunt Jackie.'

I asked Jasmine, 'Is that why we haven't seen Tameka for a while?'

Jasmine said, 'Yes, Mama, it is. I told Tameka that she knew about it and that she should have said something.'"

Eva continued, "Having that conversation with my sixteen-year-old daughter felt horrible. Not only had I been allowing Kenny to abuse me, but it had been affecting my children and their friendships. Honestly, Kellie, I already knew about Kenny and

Jackie. I just didn't say anything due to my fear of Kenny's reaction. I had confronted him before about past affairs, outside kids he has, and even his affair with Jackie, and it all ended up with arguments or some type of physical abuse."

They were all now eating, crying, and drinking wine.

Eva said, "I started to cry, and I told Jasmine to go and start packing because we would be leaving him. I called my parents that same night, told them everything, and told them that the next day while he was at work, we would be moving. I took everything from the house and decided to put it in storage until I was able to get on my feet. Without hesitation, the next day I took off from work, kept the kids out of school, and with my parents, brothers, and sisters help, we packed a rental truck and moved in with my parents. Kenny came by their house looking for me and the kids. He was angry. But, with my brothers knowing about what I had been going through, they took care of him with an old-fashioned beatdown which is exactly what he needed. When it came time for the divorce, Kenny didn't argue; he just signed the papers. He pays his child support and has no contact with the kids. I don't care what he does because I have been married to Marcus for a while now and I am finally happy. Kenny and Jackie got married and I heard she is dealing with his abusive ways now. As for Jasmine and Tameka, it took them a while, but they are back being friends. I am happy to be out of that situation."

DRINK:

_____

_____

CONVERSATION:

Have you ever been in a relationship or situation that was so bad that no matter the cost you had to leave? Did you leave, or are you still in that situation?

_____

_____

_____

_____

Join the conversation on social media at
Drinks and Conversations.

Conversation 3

What's Weight Got to Do With It

Sophia said, "Eva, I think the hardest thing about going through all this stuff is having to figure out a way to deal with it. For me, I eat. I have gained so much weight because I have been so depressed. And now, thinking about what people are saying about me since I gained the weight, I am even more depressed trying to figure out a way to drop the weight. My mama is constantly stressing me about the fact that I used to be small and skinny and now I look like I have let myself go."

Eva chimed in, "Yes, I am the same way and my mama is always saying that same thing to me too. I struggle so much with having to hear people tell me,

'You have gained a lot of weight, but you still have a pretty face.'"

Sophia said, "I understand. I hear things like, 'Once you lose weight, then you can get that good job.'"

"What does weight have to do with anything?" Camille questioned.

Kellie responded, "I think we are all dealing with this because mama does it to me too."

Sophia said, "I don't know what weight has to do with anything, but I feel like when people are used to seeing you a certain size when you are young, I guess they put in their heads that you are only pretty when you look that way."

"You know, my mama had the nerve to order me a subscription to one of those weight loss magazines. I was so pissed when I checked the mail. Of course, I look through them, but it still makes me feel like she loves me with conditions. When me and the kids were staying with them, it was like I had left one abusive relationship and went into another controlling, manipulative situation. But you know our mothers are never going to change. I mean, let me tell you, Ladies, if I got an extra chicken wing and only had two on my plate to start, she would stare at my plate. I was like, 'I cannot live like this,'" Eva said.

Kellie said, "That is wild. We know we have had crazy conversations. We have talked about those old men trying to mess around with young girls and abusive relationships, and now we are talking about the weight we all have put on and how people see us now."

"You know, I went through some things too when we were young," Camille said. "Eva and Sophia, you both know, you both were there."

Both Sophia and Eva said, "Yes, Camille, we know."

Camille turned to Kellie and said, "Don't say a word to Candace because I need to tell her on my own and I don't want her to hear it from you. I know you two are best friends, but I'm begging you, just keep it to yourself for a little while."

Kellie said, "Camille, I don't even know what you are talking about."

Eva asked, "Have you thought any more about telling her?"

By her, Eva meant Camille's daughter, Candace, that she gave birth to when they were sixteen years old.

Just then, Kellie realizes what they are talking about and says, "I promise Candace will not hear this from me."

Camille's parents were religious, in fact her father was a preacher. Camille's parents were mad when she became pregnant, but her not having the baby or giving it away was never an option. Her parents raised Candace and has Candace believing that Camille is her older sister.

Camille said, "You know, I have tried to tell her so many times and I feel like now that we are grown, I don't want her to be mad at me or my parents for keeping the truth from her all these years. Think about it, I have two other kids that she thinks are her niece and nephew."

"Camille, we know it will make you feel better if you at least talk to her," Sophia said.

Then Kellie said, "I think she might be shocked at first, but it's Candace. She is one of the most forgiving, God-fearing women we know. She will forgive you and you two will be okay."

"Yes, I agree with them," Eva said, "you need to talk to her."

Camille responded, "I am going to talk to Candace, but I'm going to talk to my mama too. I think I'm going to talk to them both at the same time. That way we can finally get it out in the open. You ladies are going to have to pray for me on this subject because I am afraid of their reactions.

Changing the subject, Camille said, "Now, about this weight thing. Yes, we are all plus size. Wait, I'm pouring more wine for this. Michael and I have been having some issues with our sex life. Now that I have retired from the military, I do feel like I have let myself go. At first, I was thinking that our issue was because we are getting older, but then I find out he has been texting and talking to some young, perky girls on social media. Now I feel like it is because of my weight."

Eva responded, "That's messed up. Mike better cut his mess out."

Kellie asked, "Why do you think it is because of your weight? Did he say that to you? Because if he did, then that's a real problem because you put that weight on having children, his children.

Sophia jumped in and said that social media has affected plenty of relationships.

"How often are you two having sex?" Eva asked.

Camille answered, "Like once every four or five months."

Sophia, Eva, and Kellie all yelled, "WHAT? That is a long time!"

Camille asked, "Sophia, how often do you and Chris have sex? And, Eva, what about you and Marc? And, Kellie, what about you and your boyfriend, Nick?"

Eva responded, "We try to do it at least once a week. But you know we are getting ready for the vow renewal, so we are really trying to save it all for the cruise.

Camille said, "Yes, we are looking forward to that cruise. Ten days in the fun and sun away from all the stress that's been going on around us."

Sophia replied, "We could use a getaway. Chris and I, we went through a drought for a while too. Even after everything he knows I went through in my life, we still had to deal with that social media thing too. I was thinking it was my weight at first, but he wanted to go to counseling because I told him I wanted a divorce. I'm not going to be with someone who wants to entertain random women in cyberspace or in the real world. I told him that I would rather be by myself than deal with another husband who is going to mistreat me."

Kellie said, "Nick and I have been doing okay; Things are going great in the sex department, plus we are looking forward to that cruise too. Things are getting serious. We have been together for over a year. I'm happy now and that's all that matters."

Eva and Camille both said to Sophia, "I did not know you two were thinking about divorce."

Sophia replied, "I was. But, of course, he was not thinking about it. After we went to counseling, talked it out, and set some new ground rules for our relationship moving forward, we have sex two to three times a week now. Divorce is off the table and our communication is much better, which was the main reason he was talking to girls over the internet. He never met any of them, and he never kissed or had sex with any other woman. I looked up every girl in his email and I emailed or called all of them. He also blocked the girls from his page. Getting everything out on the table helped us to move forward.

And now, we are happier with open communication. I would say talk to Mike and find out what is really going on with your relationship, but I don't think it is your weight at all. I think it is good to talk to someone, outside of us, to get a third-party perspective of what is going on in your relationship. And, yes, social media is messed up but you two will be alright."

DRINK:

_____

_____

CONVERSATION:

Have you ever dealt with someone harassing you about losing weight or maybe it was dropping a habit of some kind? What did you do?

_____

_____

_____

_____

Join the conversation on social media at

Drinks and Conversations.

Conversation

4

The Good Job

Eva said, "Sophia, tell us all about that craziness that has been going on at your job, because it seems like they have been causing problems pretty much since you started there."

Sophia responded, "Okay, I'll begin with how it all started with this crazy job I've been at over these past seven years."

Eva said, "Wow, yes, that's right! You have been there seven years."

"Yes, ever since I retired from the military, I had been bouncing from job to job until I landed this job," said Sophia.

Camille said, "You should have been left because we know how you don't like to get too comfortable on a regular job."

They all laughed while Eva said, "Camille, let Sophia tell her story."

They all laughed again, and Sophia said, "Yes, there is a lot to tell, but I do feel like I'm going to save some of this mess for another Drinks and Conversations Dinner. But, I will tell you ladies some of it."

She continued, "I'll start with the random day I was here at my house in the front bedroom. You know that room we turned into our office?"

They all replied, "Yes, we know exactly which room."

Sophia said, "Well, I emailed my resume to so many businesses and uploaded it to numerous employment seeking websites searching for what my mother would describe as a 'good job.' You know I only started looking for employment because remember I was back in school and hated it? You know we always had big dreams, but I knew that even though the school path might lead to me making good money it was not right for me at the time. I felt like I was on the wrong path, but you know it is hard to say no to your parents. You all know mama wanted me to be a lawyer, but we all got bit by the entrepreneurial bug when we were children and clearly our symptoms never went away.

It seemed like it took forever. I mean, I waited and waited and then finally I received a call about an interview. I went to the interview optimistic. I was upbeat, happy, and smiling. Immediately following the interview, I left with the hope of not only changing the financial future of my household, but also helping and giving back to people in need. The position I interviewed for was project manager.

The interview took place in a rented office building just before Christmas break. I met with a wonderful woman name MaryAnne. MaryAnne was the director of the program.

MaryAnne met with me and immediately fell in love. She asked me to complete a paper application because I had submitted my resume online. So, I went into the conference room next door, but I could hear her on the phone with someone. She was telling the person on the phone that she had found the perfect person for the position. When I went back into the room, she told me she would love to hire me, but they were still a few months away from opening the office I would oversee; that office was still under construction. MaryAnne told me that I was also going to have to interview with the vice president, but she said it was just a formality and that I had the job so no worries. She asked was I okay with waiting a few months to start the position. I replied, 'Yes, indeed.' I had waited for months already to get the interview, so of course I was okay with it even though I was more than ready to start making some money. Since it was right before the holiday season, Chris and I were ready to take much needed time and be with family.

After the holidays, I received the long-awaited phone call for a second interview. I had to go to the office the next day. Since the main office was two hours away, in another state, Chris decided to drive me. We arrived with plenty of time to spare and shared some laughs until the time came for me to go inside and meet my interviewer.

The interviewer's name was Jane. She was the vice president. She was friendly and informed me that she was interested in me working for the business. She requested that I go the same day and take a drug test. A week later, I received a call from the human resources director, Leslie, with the official job offer and salary amount. This came at the right time and was such a blessing for us because I was ready to start making some money. Leslie said they wanted me to start in the next couple of weeks. I had no problem with that timeline.

Let's fast forward to day one of training; I met my new co-workers. There would be four people working in my office. There was Scott, Gregory, Melissa, and me. Day one of training on the 'good job' went well as we got to know one another. At some point during that day, Leslie instructed us to all ride to work together the next day to allow the company to save money."

Eva and Camille said, "That's strange."

Kellie said, "You all had just met one another. You didn't know any of those people."

Sophia said, "Yes, I know. I was not going to do it. Melissa was going to visit one of her friends and she was not going to ride. That meant they wanted me to ride alone with men I didn't know to another state for four hours round trip. I was like NO! Well really, I was like HELL NO! I'll drive myself."

Camille said, "That's exactly what I would have said too."

Sophia continued, "We were comfortable with one another because we knew each other's names, but we weren't comfortable enough for a road trip together on day two of a new job. I felt like HR should not have been asking me to ride alone with strange men. The thought of riding alone with these two guys made me extremely uncomfortable. Nevertheless, I pulled myself together and brushed it off because, regardless, I was going to drive for my safety.

The next day for training we were on our own. The staff members who were supposed to train us were not aware of the training. There also was not another project manager for me to shadow for the new position. We struggled our way through day two despite all of the craziness.

The last day of training was simple because it was move-in day. It was our first official day in our new office. I opened the door and we all went in! The office was nice and spacious. We held a team meeting immediately. I gave everyone a copy of the key to the office along with the code to get into the building and we all decided that day we would become the best team for the entire company. Then, we set out to develop a standard for our office. As project manager of a strong team, I developed area lists and procedures for office operations. The other three contract associates started calling other businesses and making attempts to build relationships with them. We had been thrown to the wolves because our department was new and there were no guidelines that we could follow, so I had to create them for us. We became 'The Dream Team' and quickly gained recognition throughout the company as well as the entire region. There came a day when all of the divisions throughout the states met for training. This was our first meeting with everyone. Prior to that, we had only spoken on the phone or by email.

The training was provided by a training team of all African-American instructors. The CEO was a strong African-American woman named Christina. While meeting members from other states, I met a co-worker named Elizabeth. Elizabeth was a project staff member at one of the offices. Elizabeth and I were workplace cordial with one another. The team that I was overseeing was on target to meet our goal faster than any of the other teams, even though the other teams had three months head start over our team. We were only doing our jobs, but we were also making sure that we put real effort into everything we were doing. I set a new goal for my team which was to 'Be so good that nobody could ignore us.' With that motto and my stellar work ethic, attention to detail, and strong leadership abilities, we caught the attention of the executive level. I was soon given advanced duties. MaryAnne realized she had in fact hired the right person for the job and promoted me to the state liaison position, which of course came with a pay increase. Within a matter of months on the job, I became the state liaison and was tasked with creating standards for the entire state, mirroring the procedures of the division where I worked. I was now the point of contact and approving authority for the state which included securing funding for contracts. The promotion made me feel happy and strange at the same time because for years after getting out of the military, as you all remember, I had been jumping from job to job and attempting to get my business off the ground. I was finally feeling proud of myself and where I was in life at that moment.

MaryAnne sent out an official email confirming my promotion to the state liaison position. Elizabeth had been promoted to a lead contract associate position. She had the task of reviewing the contracts for approval before submitting them to me for final approval. Then, I would submit them to the business fund department to secure the funding."

Camille said, "It seemed like they realized you were more than just a pretty face and showed you that they appreciated you. I wish my job was like that. We haven't received a raise for a long time, and things have gotten worse. But, I'm going to let you finish, then I will tell you all about my situation."

Eva chimed in, "Yes, me too. I have been going through some things too."

"I have too," Kellie said, "but nothing like this."

"Ladies, it only got worse over time. I think it is time for us to really do our businesses full time," Sophia said.

Eva asked, "Sophia, what else has been happening?"

DRINK:

_____

_____

CONVERSATION:
Tell the truth, do you love your current job? Are they paying you what you are worth?

_____

_____

_____

_____

Join the conversation on social media at
Drinks and Conversations.

Conversation 5

The Hated Promotion

Sophia said, "You know, it is strange how people are cool with you until you start going up the ladder. After I was promoted, I felt a shift in the dynamic and relationship with Elizabeth. She began to act strange toward me. I was now an approving authority of her work and it caused several arguments between us. Elizabeth was telling co-workers I was just a dumb, black girl that lucked up, got hired, and ended up getting promoted for no reason. I was completely caught off guard by her actions and I didn't understand why this was suddenly coming out of left field. I felt maybe it could be that Elizabeth was finally showing her true colors. And it would appear that the relationship between us was about to change even more because I was hearing more and more of the things Elizabeth was saying behind my back to others. The main questions in my mind were, 'Is Elizabeth mad because I got promoted over her?' Or, 'Is she mad because I'm African-American and I got promoted over her?' I knew in my heart which question was correct. It would seem my workplace friend was okay if this African-American girl stayed in her place and did not excel in life.

I thought to myself that Elizabeth had another thing coming because while I only have a bachelor's degree, I have been well-educated through life lessons and reading. I showcased my skills and talents every day and I was rewarded without having to ask for a reward. Every chance Elizabeth got, she started harassing me. She even said that Leslie told her that the state liaison position I was hired for was for people who only needed to know how to use a pen and answer the phone. Elizabeth also said, 'Leslie is formally uneducated with only a GED and has worked for the business for only two years.' But Leslie is white, so her education did not make a difference because she had the right skin color.

The team members from other divisions started to look to me more for advice, assistance with their contracts, and comfort when they were feeling the wrath and harassment by Elizabeth. One of the contract associates, Sheena, said that Elizabeth only wanted to talk about me, how I got promoted, and how she feels the executive level personnel made a mistake by promoting me. Elizabeth soon became hell-bent on taking me down and she did not care who knew. She felt as though she should have been promoted over me and was starting to challenge my authority, but we officially did not work in the same department anymore as she had her own staff that she supervised through her promotion. But, she still could not get her contracts to the business finance department without my approval. I was not the only person on Elizabeth's radar. There were several individuals that she simply did not like solely based on their skin color. She had several run-ins with MaryAnne about the program, which was fueled after MaryAnne promoted me to the master's degree level position of state liaison. This action found MaryAnne on the short list of firings. Elizabeth was extremely close with the president, Edward, who would pretty much do anything she would say because the word around the water cooler was that she was sleeping with him while her husband was serving overseas in the military. I also heard through the grapevine that Elizabeth told Edward that she wanted MaryAnne gone because she had promoted me. Do you think it's a coincidence the rumor circulates and then MaryAnne gets fired by Edward? I don't think so! Rumor was also circulating that Elizabeth was trying to get him to fire me, but at that time I was the only person they sent to get the certification for the Contracts Finance Program. I was too much of an asset.

As an exit to the company, MaryAnne sent out an email to the team members with whom she wanted to keep in contact. MaryAnne really didn't explain much in her email, but she did make sure to let everyone know that she was being forced to leave. MaryAnne asked us to stay in contact with her and she said to be sure to contact her if we ever needed her for anything. The firing of MaryAnne would quickly bring a new director to take her place. But in the meantime, we went on with our work duties. Eventually the new director, Brent, came to work for the business. Brent came to my division for observation as he had heard about my team. He told me that he loved the standards I set for the teams. Brent informed me that he would like me to continue to push forward with the plan I developed. He sent out a program-wide email to let the entire team, which included Elizabeth, know that anything that came from me was the same as if the information or questions were directly coming from him.

Shortly after Brent came to work for the business, there was the addition of a new team member to one of the teams. Her name was Maggie. I had the task of training new team members on the acceptable standards which I developed for the program. On the first day of Maggie's training, she came to my division. On the second day, I went to her division to train her in her work environment. Maggie was a quick study and caught on to the computer portion with ease. As I trained Maggie, she disclosed to me that on her first day of work, Elizabeth was talking about me saying that I was a dumb, black girl and that I have everyone fooled because I don't really know much about the contracts. Maggie went on to say that Elizabeth told her that whatever she doesn't understand or whatever I don't train her on, she should come to her for anything she needs.

Maggie said she had informed Elizabeth that she was married to an African-American man and her children were African-American and that she didn't think that it was right for her to be bashing someone who is not there to defend themselves. Maggie told Elizabeth that furthermore the color of a person's skin should not make a difference in the amount of knowledge they possess. Maggie said she informed Leslie of what Elizabeth said and Leslie said they would handle it. I knew nothing would happen because I had already spoken with Leslie about Elizabeth's behavior and nothing happened. Maggie said she was letting me know because it was the right thing to do."

Camille said, "Girl, I would have to give Elizabeth a good beat down."

"Yes, I'm with Camille," Kellie said.

Eva said, "Sophia, I think you been doing the right thing. I mean, don't let anyone treat you a certain way. But, we know that you know how to handle yourself."

Sophia responded, "That place has only grown worse over the years."

DRINK:

_____

_____

CONVERSATION:
Have you ever disliked a co-worker or had a co-worker who disliked you? What happened?

_____

_____

_____

_____

Join the conversation on social media at
Drinks and Conversations.

Conversation 6

Let the Games Begin

Sophia said, "Shortly after Maggie informed me of this information, Elizabeth came into the conference room and said that Leslie wanted to speak with us. Us being Elizabeth and myself, and that they are having an emergency meeting right now. I went down the hall, following Elizabeth slowly as I did not know what I was walking into because of course I don't trust Elizabeth. In addition to that, I was mad after hearing what Maggie had just told me. Elizabeth got to the end of the hallway, opened the door, and entered the president's office. I entered slowly to be greeted by Brent, Edward, and Leslie. At that point, I felt completely set up plus the fires of hell were already sparked inside of me because of my conversation with Maggie. Surprisingly, the meeting had nothing to do with me. They were holding the meeting because they were trying to get rid of Nancy. I looked at them confused and asked, 'What do you mean get rid of her?' The reply in the room was, 'We know that you are her supervisor, so we are coming to you because while we of course can just fire her, we would rather it be for a reason and have a paper trail so that we won't have to worry about her going to file a lawsuit against us. She has already pulled the race card on us before and we don't want to run into that again.' I looked at each one of them and said, 'You all know I'm African-American too, right? This is crazy and I cannot and will not participate in setting up someone, who is trying to work to make a living to provide for their family, to get fired.'"

Camille said, "Hold up! So, they were plotting to fire somebody and wanted you to be a part of it?"

Sophia responded, "Yes, Girl. I never had first-hand knowledge how cut-throat white people really are. I told them you all allow Elizabeth to continue to harass and be racist towards people. I made sure to let Leslie know that Maggie told me what Elizabeth said about me. I told them, 'You all are interesting and crazy too if you think I am going to do this. I have a team member to train.' I got up and Leslie told me, 'It would be in your best interest to keep this conversation between us.' I stared at her, said nothing, left the room, and went back to training Maggie. I was concerned about my job at that point because they had let me into their secret Illuminati-style meeting with the hope that I would join their club, but I didn't and never will. I decided to say nothing at that time and went on about my business until I left. I did call Nancy on my drive back home and left it in her hands.

Everything was going smooth for a while, but a few weeks afterward it would seem that I had become the target once again for Elizabeth. She began with her harassment again and started telling certain co-workers that I was not going to be there for long. I was catching many mistakes on their contracts, which is supposed to be Elizabeth's job, but because I was having to send things back more and more it looked like she was not doing her job. I felt she was spending too much time focusing on me and not enough time checking her work.

On another training day, Elizabeth said, 'Let's play a game.' Brent had just left our meeting to head to another meeting, but perhaps that is the reason why Elizabeth wanted to play such a foolish game. I felt that it must be her essence of white privilege that made her feel some type of way about me now, or could it be the always present racist tone throughout the entire business? They had even fired the all African-American training team MaryAnne had hired. They said it was because they didn't want to renew their contract because they cost too much, but I guess they forgot that I was in the meeting when they said they didn't like them and wanted to get rid of them. They felt as though they could find some white trainers because they believed the black trainers were not worth the money."

Camille said, "Sophia, I am fuming. You have been dealing with this all this time and you haven't been saying anything."

Sophia responded, "We as black people get caught up in the fact that we have landed the so-called 'good job,' but we don't realize what is really going on around us. We need to step back and pay attention. So, back to the meeting. It became clear to me that Elizabeth had conspired with some of the other white employees prior to this meeting. She said, 'Since Brent isn't here, we should go around the room and say what we don't like about the program. This way it is out in the open and we can see if we can fix our issues amongst ourselves.' I protested the idea because something like that should be done anonymously. Elizabeth and I engaged in a heated argument. We all decided to take a vote and the majority of the team agreed they were okay with having an open discussion. The agreement was that everything said was to be constructive criticism only about the job; there would be no bashing or degrading of anyone.

We started going around the room and the team members began to say what they don't like about the program. I realized that quite a few people, white people, said they felt that I only correct the mistakes on the contracts of the African-Americans and that when they make a mistake I send it back to them so they can fix it. They also said that when I send them an email, I am aggressive in tone to them and they feel that it is because they are white. I immediately addressed the issues with each person who brought up an issue with me. I looked at Elizabeth and saw a devilish smirk on her face as if she was thinking her plan had come together perfectly.

At the end of the meeting, I went to Brent's office and spoke with him about the discussion. He seemed annoyed by me wanting to talk about the meeting. I also emailed Leslie after the incident, but she was unavailable to meet with me about the harassment I had been going through. Leslie said she would get back with me about a meeting date and time. A few days had passed by and how I was being targeted was weighing heavily on me, plus Leslie was yet to get back to me about a meeting. I decided to address the situation head on. I sent out an email to the entire department addressing the issue from co-workers who said that I was only assisting the African-American co-workers. I made sure to copy Leslie, Brent, and Edward in the email. After I sent that email, I began to get emails and phone calls from other co-workers saying they had been having some concerns with Elizabeth also and had tried to address them with the executive level and they were not taken seriously either. I listened to their concerns and took notes with the hope of having a meeting with the executive level and getting the opportunity to voice my complaints. Then, I would also voice the concerns of others who trusted me.

A day later, I received an email from Kayla, the receptionist, about the meeting. Kayla asked if I could meet Brent, Edward, and Leslie at the Applebee's restaurant to speak about the concerns. This seemed strange as the office was ten floors high with plenty of conference rooms for meeting space, but I agreed and met with the executive level at the Applebee's. I spoke about the harassment that I had been experiencing as well as the concerns of the other team members. They informed me that they would handle the situation, but at the same time appeared not to really care about the situation.

A few days later, there was a meeting for the team and Elizabeth was missing. It turns out that Leslie had a conversation with Elizabeth and told her that I had officially filed a complaint against her through HR. Elizabeth was not off due to corrective action; she had in fact just taken some days off from work.

Considering this, I made the decision to go to a higher authority of officials to file a complaint and was also met with no help. They informed me that while it was wrong for Leslie to disclose my name to Elizabeth, it was not against the law. They also informed me that since most of the harassment was verbal, it would be hard to prove and win a case. After I attempted to do the right thing by informing HR and the officials, with failure on both ends, I decided to just go about my business and do my work because one thing about people like Elizabeth is they don't stop with their evil ways. As the phrase goes, 'A leopard never changes his spots.' She would be back at it soon. And when the time came, I knew just how to handle her—straightforward!"

DRINK:

_____

_____

CONVERSATION:
Have you ever dealt with some type of harassment in the workplace? Did you inform HR? What happened?

_____

_____

_____

_____

Join the conversation on social media at
Drinks and Conversations.

Conversation 7

The Change Up

Sophia continued, "Like clockwork, Elizabeth was right back on track harassing employees. This time it was Nancy again, along with Lauren, Annie, and Renee. Of course, they were all African-American, no need to ask! Elizabeth was constantly getting into verbal arguments and email disputes with one or all of them. Nancy as you all remember is the lady Elizabeth was trying to get me to set up to get her fired. Nancy had been taking extensive notes and recordings of all conversations with Elizabeth because I had given her the heads up on the situation. Elizabeth took it upon herself to inform Leslie that these ladies were being aggressive with her even though she was the aggressor. Elizabeth was conveniently leaving out the fact that she was constantly instigating situations. When Leslie asked them to come to her office, they each had a notebook and recordings of the things Elizabeth had been doing or saying to them along with the date and time. Leslie was mad because the executive level thought they finally had a good reason to get rid of Nancy, but they had nothing on any of them. Therefore, all of the ladies went back to work and of course nothing was done to Elizabeth, even with the evidence at hand.

The executive level decided to hold our monthly meeting the same day as the yearly party to ensure that everyone was at the main office. As everyone went to the large conference room for the party, Brent pulled Lauren aside and asked her to come to his office. When Lauren finally made it to the party, she was extremely mad because Brent had just written her up for going back and forth with Elizabeth via email. I warned Lauren about what they were trying to do. I informed her that Leslie told me how the company handles terminations is that they would not just fire someone. There would be some type of corrective action or write-ups before they just fire someone, unless there was some type of fraud or something that they could not overlook. Lauren said to me, 'So I guess it's safe to say they are after me.' I replied, 'Yes, and I honestly believe they are after the both of us.'

The week following brought on much drama at our division. Scott and Gregory had a thing for talking about the girls they were messing around with, well mainly it was Scott because Gregory was married. But we were all still amused by Scott and his stories that we believed were mostly made up. Renee came to my office and said she was offended by Scott always talking about the girls he was messing with. I asked her if she wanted me to call him into my office. Her response was something I was not expecting. She said, 'No, I will just talk with him about it.' At that point, I was confused. I said, 'You're going to talk to him?' She said, 'Yes, you know we are together, right?' And I said, 'No, how would I know that?' I asked her were the two of them exclusive and she said she didn't know and that she had spent several weekends at his place. I said, 'Maybe the two of you need to have a conversation outside of the office with clothes on and see what you two are really doing because it seems like you might be dating him, but he is not dating you.' She said, 'Well, yes, you are right and I'm tired of him disrespecting me.' I didn't even know what to say. She said, 'Thank you.' And while I was thinking about what to say to HR, since she initially came with a complaint but then told me she was only mad because they were sleeping together, I received a phone call from HR wanting to know what was going on in my division. I told HR what I knew and left it at that. On the way home, I laughed hard about the situation because how can you be mad if you two never established the terms of what you were doing? That put me in the middle of a lover's situation that was going on right under my nose.

My previous thought of not getting involved with drama quickly became a distant memory. My division had a contract with a man named David, a white racist client, who lived in our service area and happened to also be friends with Elizabeth. Gregory was assigned David's case to assist with his potential business contract. David immediately voiced his complaint saying that he did not want to work with Gregory. I explained to David the business contracts were taken care of as they came in, not by who you prefer to work with and definitely not because you do not want to work with a person of a certain race, which is discrimination and racism and has no place here. I also informed David that he was there for another reason and not to make friends. Soon it became apparent to Gregory that Elizabeth was guiding David's contract. David told Gregory that he knew the entire breakdown of how we would help him with getting his business off the ground because Elizabeth had told him. Gregory tried to speak with Elizabeth about the matter, but she ignored him while saying that David was a friend and she was not helping him in any way. Gregory also came to me with the situation. I had already spoken with David about the matter and was not going to speak with Elizabeth about it as he was not in her service area; therefore, Elizabeth went to Brent about the issue. I informed Brent of the situation and he said there was really nothing we could do about them talking. I reminded Brent that it was a conflict of interest as well as unethical for her to do these things, but Brent insisted it was not an issue. Brent also said he wanted to change the contract associate from Gregory to Scott so that David would feel comfortable, thus encouraging his racist ways.

It was an action that anyone could have seen coming. Racism at its finest.

Gregory and I did not worry about it because we knew the encouragement of racism would happen. In the end, Scott was not able to take David's contract because he had such a huge case log, and there were no other contract associates who could take his case either. So, he had to go back to Gregory's log. There was now some tension between David and Gregory. Elizabeth continued to be a huge part of the equation and Gregory struggled to get David on a positive track. Gregory's other contracts were moving forward and getting their lives in motion, but David was being coached from the sidelines by Elizabeth which was really making things so much worse. David came to the point where he exhausted all of his assistance and was not making payments on his contract himself; we were making them for him. Meanwhile, Gregory also had a young African-American mother, Rachel, with a one-month old newborn daughter. Rachel submitted an application for review for a different type of assistance for a business contract. She was refused because when she completed her application she was missing some needed documents. She said that she was unable to get the information because she had recently left her husband and was trying to get her life on track. Rachel said that her husband had torn up most of her important papers. Since she was from another state, she would have to order her documents from that state.

Because we could not help her through our business, I was making some calls to try to get her help through other sources in our building to possibly get her documents. I went to Brent and Edward about speaking with one of the other businesses in the building, but Rachel did not get any help. Rachel ended up moving back home to Oregon and finally has her business.

While all of this was going on, Elizabeth managed to obtain approval for more assistance to help with David's contract by asking Edward to speak with one of the other businesses in the building, which is the same thing that I had done and was met with 'no way' for an answer. Gregory and I were not even mad because there were constant tones of racism and discrimination in our workplace."

Camille said, "Your job has a lot going on."

Kellie said, "I'm telling you, Sis, I would have to leave that job before I hurt someone."

"Ladies, it gets better," Sophia said.

They all started laughing.

Eva said, "This is some real craziness you have been dealing with. They are for real racist."

Sophia responded, "I had grown tired of fighting with them because I had raised the issue to the highest level and had still been met with no help on the matter. On that same day, our team ended the year with a small meal at our division and we went our separate ways. We all hoped the upcoming year would bring a better workplace and morale at the respective divisions and at the business. We hoped the next two weeks of vacation would bring the opportunity to get much needed time off from work to be away from all the ups, downs, drama, racist comments, discrimination, and all out lies experienced at the business. We were just happy that we made it to the end of the year with our jobs.

That very night when I got home from work, I flopped on the couch mad as hell as usual at another day of the racist ways I had been enduring. I was so happy it was Christmas break!

Chris took a long, deep breath and said, 'Here we go again. Why do you let them stress you so much?'

I told him, 'This job is not supposed to be this hard.'

He responded, 'Those people at your job are only like this because they know that you know more than they do. Think about it. They are always asking you questions about the contracts and they don't know anything about some of the other forms. What we really need to focus on is our business so that one day you can go into work and tell them you are done and then you won't have to worry about them anymore.'

The new year brought more change in that they fired four black people in one day. Of course, you know it was Nancy, Annie, Renee, and Lauren. They also changed my position in the company. The executive level did what they wanted to do because we were all black. Elizabeth was finally getting what she wanted and that was firing Nancy. Renee got fired because she filed the harassment suit on the white worker Scott. Lauren got fired because she would not stop going back and forth with Elizabeth. Annie was just a black girl that they didn't like; they had expressed in several executive level meetings that they thought she was incompetent.

Soon, we had to hire someone new at our office. There was a young African-American lady named Cassandra, we called her Cassie. She was a friend of ours who used to work in the office building next door and she had recently lost her job. Once the job posted, we told her about it and how to submit. Elizabeth had in her mind that she wanted my office to have a white girl that she knew but who did not know the job. On the day of the interview, Brent and I interviewed several ladies including Cassie. A week later, Edward showed up at my office and said he was there to do the second interview with Cassie. I told Gregory to call Cassie and let her know so that she could come to the interview. While Gregory made the call, I talked Cassie up to Edward. It turned out that Elizabeth told Edward that he had an interview knowing that Cassie would not show because she didn't know about the meeting. It was a set-up. Well, the joke was on her because Cassie showed up and got the job.

A few months later, Brent decided to retire and that brought a new breed of backstabbing leadership… inexperienced females. There was an African-American man named Steven who had worked there for twelve years. He applied for the position of director in an effort to gain some growth in the company, but they didn't even interview him for the position. In fact, Steven kept looking for the job posting and it never showed up because they never even posted it. Steven only knew about the job opening because Brent told him he was retiring. They brought in an inexperienced white female, Sandra, whom they had promised the job. Soon after she was hired, she helped her friends get hired. She hired associate director, Dora, and managing director, Emma. She was in the market of creating jobs for her friends and with ninety percent of the employees being African-American, no lie, the very first email she sent out to everyone inquired about education levels. It really didn't matter because there were no African-American employees in senior level positions of the company higher than the state liaison position. After she got the information she was seeking, then came the shake-ups. My position was dissolved at my work location and moved to another city. There was no warning, just a phone call that said, 'We are changing you to another department.' Ultimately, Steven filed a discrimination lawsuit against them and won big.

The new all-female leadership were all friends and they quickly got into a who's the better female contest. Sandra was hired first. She brought on Dora who eventually back-stabbed her; now Dora is Sandra's boss. It appears that Sandra didn't learn her lesson because her friend Emma seems to be on track to get her job now. They are a horrible group of women. These ladies constantly send aggressive and threatening emails and talk down to people like we are beneath them. The only good thing they did was fire Elizabeth. They didn't like her because they wanted their friends to be in the positions."

Camille said, "That's messed up, Sophia."

Eva chimed in, "I don't know how you have put up with them this long."

Sophia responded, "Well, I used to like the job, but now it is just that—a job."

DRINK:

_____

_____

CONVERSATION:
Did you ever have a supervisor who was okay to work with who then became leadership but did not have the ability to actually lead? What happened?

_____

_____

_____

_____

Join the conversation on social media at
Drinks and Conversations.

Conversation

8

No More Growth

Sophia said, "After the executive level changed my position, Gregory became head of our office. I was still doing liaison work, but just for my area not the state. Gregory learned my passcode, went into my system, ordered some things, falsified notes, and added my electronic signature to them. He was fired. Now the same thing recently happened to me again. This time, Emma went into my system, ordered some items, made notes about it, and electronically placed my signature. She still has her job and they refuse to fire her, even after I reported her to Human Resources (which was the same thing I had done with Gregory because I didn't want them looking at me like I did something). I don't care who you are, wrong is wrong, especially when it comes to using me to do your dirty work."

Camille said, "So, the white girl, Emma, they are letting her get away with it?"

"Yes," Sophia said, "Even though I have evidence, they have basically just swept it under the rug."

Camille said, "I'm going to pour me another glass of wine for this. Who else needs wine?"

The ladies all replied with "I do."

Camille lined up the glasses and poured all of the ladies a fresh glass of wine.

Sophia continued, "The worst thing about the situation with Gregory was that once he got fired, his position was up for grabs and they posted the job. I applied and Sandra gave me a half-assed interview because she was more concerned with my mental state—how I was in the Air Force and do I currently see a therapist—than my ability to perform as a leader, which I had already shown for years that I can do successfully. The interview only lasted a few short minutes and then she wanted to go over case logs. I told her that what she was trying to talk about had nothing to do with the interview. I asked her when

I would hear something about the job. She told me that she was going to find another candidate. I just told her okay because I could already tell by the way she interviewed me and was acting that they were not going to hire me. Cassie also interviewed for the job. We have both been there for many years and we both have bachelor's degrees. The position preferred someone with a master's degree, but I had already held a position in the company that was master's level. Either one of us should've been a good candidate. A few weeks later, they interviewed a few other candidates for the position. I could hear everything through my office wall. This time it was a two-person interview with Emma, something Cassie and I did not receive. They also did not ask any of the other candidates about their mental health.

A few weeks after that, Sandra came to me and said that they hired someone for the state liaison position. I asked why I did not get the job and her response was that they were requiring the state liaison to have a master's degree and she hoped that not getting the position wouldn't affect my anxiety or work ethic. There was nothing I could do but understand because I don't have a master's degree and neither did Cassie. I put it out of my head and went on about my work as usual. But, it was strange that, somehow, I no longer qualified for a position that I held for three years and the qualifications changed from preferred to required after Cassie and I were interviewed.

The new state liaison, Heather, started work and she was filled with issues. She was a white girl, of course, going through a divorce. She had four kids and had to get a new place to stay. She was constantly asking Cassie and myself to help her with issues she was having with the contracts. Sandra and Emma went so far as wanting us to do her work for her. Of course, I told them no."

Camille said, "I would tell her hell no!"

Sophia continued on, "Heather said that Sandra and Emma told her that Cassie and I know this job better than anyone working at the business and if she needed any help to ask us. It's interesting how they wanted us to help her out, but neither of us was good enough to be in the position. Keep in mind, a position that I was already in. And if I was doing a bad job, then I would have been fired a long time ago. But no, I received all types of awards and letters of appreciation for my work in that position. Within three weeks of being on the job, Heather had a nervous breakdown and had to take a few days off from work because she was so stressed out, but there were so many concerns about me and my mental health. When she returned, she told Cassie and I that she was stressed out and needed to get herself together. She said that she had never received so many emails before on a job. She also said that she was going to start seeing a therapist. As the three of us talked, Heather also shared some information about her life, her past employment, and most importantly her education level. She, in fact, did not have a master's degree. For me to discover that Heather was now certified, by her own admission, as not being more qualified for the position than either Cassie or myself was the straw that broke the camel's back. I had to come to the realization that I had been discriminated against, and it hurt. I worked so hard for seven years and gave so much to the company that to be treated in such a way was an insult and a metaphorical slap in the face. While all of that had been going on at my division, a black lady from another division decided she had enough of it. She quit, and they replaced her with an inexperienced and unqualified white lady. It seems to be the pattern, as it does not matter if the person is qualified for a position because the only quality a person must possess is the right skin color. There's no more growth for me because they are making sure this smart, black girl goes no further in this business, which is discrimination.

Eva asked, "Sophia, what did you do?

Camille said, "What are you going to do?"

Kellie chimed in, "This is messed up for real."

Sophia replied, "I have a case pending against them. I just have to wait to see what happens. I really can't go into details. In the meantime, I have walked away from the company to pursue my business full-time and hopefully help others by letting them know that they don't have to put up with discrimination and racism in the workplace."

DRINK:

_____

_____

CONVERSATION:
Have you ever attempted to get a promotion, only to get passed over for someone else? Did you understand why you were not chosen? Did you feel like you deserved the position? Did you feel like they held you back from growing within the company?

_____

_____

_____

_____

Join the conversation on social media at
Drinks and Conversations.

Conversation
9

Forgiving Wooden Nickels

Eva said, "I tell you all, the worst part about my job was having to deal with all the criminals coming into the office. Some of them are sex offenders. My boss knows they did it, but once they hire him, he is sworn to defend them. Some of them came into the office and called themselves trying to sweet talk me. I was like, even if I was not married, I would still not want any of them. I had a hard time watching some of them get away with what they have done, especially the ones who we know are guilty. It was a job, so I guess I had to suffer through it until my business started to grow."

All the ladies looked at Eva and wanted to know why she was speaking of her job in the past tense.

Camille asked, "Eva, did you quit your job?"

Eva responded, "No, I did not quit, he let me go after all these years. The attorney I worked for is going through a nasty divorce because he has been sleeping with the perky little white girl paralegal at our office. And now he must downsize. He is only keeping her for obvious reasons. So, I am going to have to get my business into full gear too. It really pisses me off how easily these white people can smile in your face, fire you, then go to lunch like you mean nothing to them. I was there for him when he first became an attorney and opened the doors to his office, and I have been a faithful employee for all these years. Now, I am without a job. I am glad that Marc works so we are not going to be in a situation, but it is still messed up the way they treat us. Don't get me wrong, I enjoyed being a paralegal and making money. But, I am not all together mad because I really want to run my own business, set my own hours, and most importantly set my own wage and not have to accept the scraps I'm given. I had to wait a whole year to see any type of pay increase, and even then it was pennies or pretty much nothing because every year the insurance goes up which quickly dissolves those pennies he was proudly giving as a raise. I am hoping with the business ideas we have that we can come together and build an empire."

Sophia responded, "That is messed up because you have been with him for a long time."

"I'm not worried about it because God will provide, and we will be alright," Eva said.

They all agreed that God will always make a way.

Camille said, "I am in the same boat as you two right now. The other day, the store owner said she wanted to see me. So, I was thinking it was going to be about the general manager position because they have not filled the position since our general manager of the store retired. Them not filling the position seemed strange, but I figured they were trying to decide who they were going to put in it. So, I went to the store owner's office and she told me they were downsizing the store and would be moving to a smaller building, but they would not be taking all the employees with them. And then came the boom. They were only going to have two managers and I was not going to be one of them. She said that they are going to be able to pay two younger ladies less than what they are paying just for me in salary and they have to save on their overhead right now. You two are right, these white business owners feel like they can treat us any kind of way and we must accept it. I really need to get my business going hard and fast too because I like to have my own money."

Just then Eva said, "I'm going to run to the restroom."

Eva went into the other room only to make a phone call to Candace. She asked Candace if she was coming to the house. Candace said that she would try her best to make it. Eva headed back into the room with Camille, Kellie, and Sophia. Unbeknownst to them, she had called Camille's daughter to come over for an intervention.

Eva said, "Now that we all are about to be jobless, what are we going to do? It's time for us to make this happen!"

Sometime during the extended Drinks and Conversations Dinner, Eva received a text message from Candace saying that she was no longer going to be able to make it. Eva responded to her saying it was alright and they could meet up at another time.

Kellie said, "I haven't lost my job yet, but they are getting on my last nerve. I am ready to get things going with my makeup business. My clientele has grown, and Nick has been saying I need to do it more as a business rather than working at the store selling cosmetics for someone else. I'm in on whatever the plan is going to be."

Sophia took Eva, Camille, and Kellie's hands and said, "The first thing that I must do is say this, I forgive anyone who has ever done something to me. I also ask for the forgiveness of God for the things that I have done wrong in my life. And as of this day, I plan to take my wooden nickels and use them as tools for me to move forward and build something great for myself, my family, and my friends. I ask that you all, my sisters, forgive me for not letting you into my life more and for keeping these secrets from you."

They clenched their hands together tighter and Kellie said, "We all are sisters, of course we forgive you. We will always love you." Eva and Camille agreed.

Eva prayed, "I am forgiving those who have harmed me and those whom I have harmed, and I ask for the grace of God to shine on me, my family, and my friends in our time of need."

"I know I still have one more wooden nickel that I am working on, but I do forgive those who have wished bad on me and I ask for forgiveness from God and from Candace, once I tell her that I am her mother. I also ask for the strength to tell her in the first place," Camille prayed.

Kellie prayed, "I forgive those who have done me wrong and I ask for the forgiveness of God for all the things I have done wrong in my life."

Sophia said, "We also ask for blessings for all of our future business endeavors. We ask all of these things in Jesus' name."

All of the ladies together said, "Amen."

After their group prayer, they all agreed that since they were already working together on some events and weddings—along with Camille's daughter, Candace, as a photographer—they would make it official and form a wedding and event planning business.

Camille asked, "What are we going to call our business?"

Sophia responded, "What if we use our initials. CESK Events. We know Candace will be in with us too, but there is no point in having two C's. Plus, people can say CESK. It is like desk, but with a C.

They all looked at each other with smiles on their faces and said, "We love it!"

DRINK:

_____

_____

CONVERSATION:
What are your goals or dreams you would like to achieve? What are you going to do to reach them?

_____

_____

_____

_____

Join the conversation on social media at
Drinks and Conversations.

Conversation 10

Time to Step Out and Receive Everything Life Brings

Eva said, "I am ready. I believe that we must claim our dreams before they even come to pass, because we as black people spend most of our lives chasing the money instead of pursuing the dream. We are conditioned to work for others, so we get that 'good job' and have all these dreams that we don't follow. I believe that we should follow our destiny. Lately, when people ask me what I do, I have been telling them that I bake wedding cakes. I have also been passing out my cards to a lot of people because I believe that I have my own business and, hell, I am a business owner!"

Camille said, "Many people don't like to follow their dreams because of fear. They don't share their dreams and visions with family and friends for fear of ridicule because let's be honest, we as black people don't support each other the way other races do. Like at our jobs, look at how they bring in their people to take our places. They know less than us and are less qualified for a job, but they help each other by any means necessary, especially to the detriment of a black person. They know that nine and a half times out of ten the black person is not going to fight back because we are just happy to have a job."

Sophia chimed in, "Yes, we must be willing to Step Out and Receive Everything Life Brings, which is what God has planned for us. We had to start by developing our talents, now we must be willing to put in a lot of work and we already know a lot of free hours. The first thing we need to do is decide where we want to go with this business. Are we hoping to just make money or are we wanting to make a difference?"

"Ladies, it is two in the morning and we have been doing Drinks and Conversations all night. How about we take some time to write down our thoughts and ideas and come back together in the light of day and really pull this together," said Eva.

They all agreed. Camille, Eva, and Kellie asked Sophia if she wanted any help cleaning up.

Sophia said, "No, we ate everything so there are only dirty dishes. I'll get them when the sun comes up."

As the ladies headed toward the door, Sophia told everyone, "You better send out a group text when you make it home."

Sophia made her way to her bedroom, showered, and watched television until she received the group text from each of the ladies. Then, she leaned over, kissed Chris, and went to sleep.

Over the next few days, the ladies worked at getting their ideas together and registered their business name with the state over the internet. That Monday, they went to officially register their business at the courthouse, and this time they had Candace with them. CESK Events, LLC was officially formed.

Over the next few months, they worked late nights and discussed many aspects of their business. Camille was still going back and forth on when or how to tell Candace that she is her mother.

The next Drinks and Conversations Dinner was at Eva's and it doubled as a business meeting.

Camille said, "You know we are going to need to soak up every aspect of information about our desired goals."

All of the ladies were now equal partners in the event planning industry, and they were quickly becoming the most sought-after event planning company in the area.

Sophia started talking to the ladies about the importance of all of them appreciating their talents and learning how to work together not just as friends, but also as strong black women.

"Appreciating our talents is a major part of our success plan and it seems like it should be easy but it's not. We all have been blessed with a gift from God; we are able to do a variety of things, but we must appreciate our talents that God has given to us. We must make sure to never lose hope during the chaos that is going to come our way. We all walked away or were pushed away from stressful job environments, but it is still going to take each one of us to do our parts, along with being accountable and taking responsibility for ourselves during our growth process," Sophia said.

She continued on, "I know we can make this business a success. I feel empowered. If they wouldn't have tried their best to break me down at my job, I would have never known that I'm unbreakable. The executive level is seeing the mistakes they made now. After I left, some other black people also left the company, which means they are unbreakable too. And so are you! I feel the time is now for us to create together and not compete with one another. When I told my mama about what was going on at my job and how they were discriminating against me and others, her response was, 'That is the way it is; nothing is going to change. It's going to be that way until the end of time.' My response to her was, 'I will never be a workplace slave and I will never accept mistreatment until the end of time.' I told her that God has given me many gifts, including discernment. Then I told her, 'The Lord will grant that the enemies who rise up against me will be defeated before me.'

I know that we all have some huge mountains to climb to reach our goals, but I also know that there is nothing in this world that cannot be moved out of my way in order for me to reach my goals and fulfill God's will.

God gives us our dreams in the form of seeds planted within us, and we know that God would not give us the dream without surrounding us with the resources to achieve the dream. I believe He puts everything in our lives to make our dreams happen. Everything is within our reach... the right places, the right time, and the right people. Look at our situations. All of us have been through so much in our lives and with our jobs, yet we found a way to come together as black women and build and grow a business. We all know that there are forces that are against us though, right?"

Camille responded, "Yes, I know. There are so many people starting to hate on us now that we are doing more and more weddings and events."

"Yes, that is true," Eva agreed.

Sophia said, "I understand that, but I'm talking about the forces within us."

Candace interrupted saying, "I have to leave and go see a friend."

Eva continued the conversation saying, "I read somewhere that success breeds success. I take that to mean that we all are successful women in our own right, so if we continue to come together and offer quality products at affordable prices, we will be successful and continue to grow. This is finally our time to shine. It's time to show off our hard work and our perseverance; it's time to stop collecting wooden nickels. I am happy that we have made the decision to actively pursue our dreams. By the way Camille, have you said anything to Candace yet?"

Camille said, "I did speak with her along with my mother and Candace said she already knew. She said she has known for years. She says she is not mad. She forgives me, and she loves me."

"We know you were scared," Eva said, "We knew you would talk to her when you were ready."

Camille replied, "I am happy that I got it out of the way and said something to her. I feel like we have a stronger relationship now that I am not carrying that secret, even though she already knew because she figured it out on her own. So, Ladies, I got rid of my last wooden nickel."

Kellie said, "I told you that Candace would forgive you."

Eva said, "I am happy for you."

Sophia said, "That is wonderful, Camille, I am so happy for you."

Camille continued, "All of us are strong black women who have gone through a lot over the course of our lives. We have shared our faults and failures with one another and now we are able to share the gifts we have received from God. There was one day at church when my dad was preaching that always sits in my mind. He said that we all have been blessed with gifts and talents but some people do not believe that so they let their fires burn out. But, if we believe in our gifts and work hard, even the lowest man can rise beyond the heavens and collect the rewards.

Sophia, I want to tell you to be encouraged. I know it has been very difficult for you lately. Remember that job was only funding your future. You are too intelligent and too valuable for that place. God has a big mission for you and for us. Nothing that has happened to you or anything you are going through now is in vain. Even though it seems as if your enemies are winning… they are not! The wicked games that people play do not prosper! Eventually their way will be clouded, and they will receive what they have planted. God has put you and all of us on a new journey to grow our brands and businesses. Transition is often started with challenge and frustration because we are creatures of comfort and habit. Sometimes there must be an irritant that makes us uncomfortable so that we reach farther and reach for the Father. He has us in the palm of His hands, my sister. He will not fail us. He sees in the dark. There was something dark in the place where you worked, and He wants only light for you. You must remember that He will not allow you to fall or fail. We are both tall girls and... do you remember how growing used to hurt just a little when we were young? But when it was over, we were okay. Your growing pains are worth the desired outcome. These challenges are just blessings in disguise. We have already won my sister and friend."

Sophia said "Yes, I believe that. I believe that our true happiness and fulfillment begins when we take control of our gifts and allow God to use us. I have felt almost like a slave to my work over the past few years and I have been yearning for the feeling of wholeness. I used to be a person who loved my job; I brought it home with me. And I got into plenty of arguments with Chris because I thought I had to be bi-living and be able to operate in any setting to keep people impressed with me and to keep my job. And when I say bi-living, I mean speak proper English, follow through on all assignments, and not be late to be on the white level. And be a little bit late and use slang at times to be on the black level. And when in the company of both, just speak only when spoken to in order to get through the setting. The white people that I was trying to impress to keep my so-called 'good job' went out of their way to lie, backstab, and do whatever it took to keep this black girl in her place and only let me get so far in the company, because God forbid a black girl with less education than a white person know more or be in command of an entire project. No, instead, let's bring in a less qualified white girl and make that black girl train her because that black girl is our strongest asset and internal resource. That's why we can't let her go. I guess they said not on their watch. And when that happened, my passion for the job disappeared because they put a cap on my growth. The best thing to do when something like that happens is to make sure to keep a smile on your face because it will confuse the hell out of your enemies. They will never see what is coming.

I know we have spent our lives taking and collecting wooden nickels and we have a nice collection of them, but I believe that we can turn them into something beautiful like CESK Events. It doesn't matter to me if we have to reinvent ourselves, let's do it because I think the people who are unsuccessful are the people who are trying to take the easy road to get to success fast. I think some people work based on how they feel rather than the real value of the dream journey. I don't want that to be us. I'm happy that we are trying our best to get rid of our wooden nickels, build something beautiful, and of course trust what God has for us. To reach those goals, we have to nurture and protect our genuine characters and values. And through the grace of God, I know we will be successful."

Sophia continued, "Ladies, we are in the process of believing in something that we cannot see and that's called faith! Let's continue to SOAR while we step out on faith to receive everything life brings!"

The ladies stood up, gave each other hugs, and told one another that they were looking forward to taking CESK Events to the next level, seeing one another more, and having more discussions at the next Drinks and Conversations Dinner.

Acknowledgments

I would like to acknowledge GOD, first and foremost. I thank you, GOD, for every breath that I breathe and for keeping the fire for business and helping others burning within me. Even when I tried to put it out, You made sure the flame stayed lit. I want to thank my readers, The Achievers, for supporting this vision. I hope your minds and hearts have been opened more after reading *Collecting Wooden Nickels* and that my words become like fertilizer in your world to offer you strength and determination for your family, in your business, and throughout your life. I would like to thank my parents, Larry and Rose Ann Mosley. You two have supported my every move. Even when you knew some of them were bad moves, you allowed me the chance to fall on my own so that I would know how to get back up and still be okay. You two have always been ready to help me just in case. I thank you for always, always, always being there. I love you two more than my words could ever say! I want to thank my uncle, Lawyer Lilly Sr., for all the times when I needed someone to listen to me. You have always been more like a big brother than an uncle to me. I love you!

I thank my brother and sister-in law, Larry and Charletha Mosley, for your neverending support in all of my adventures. I love you! Thank you to my nieces, London Yvonne and Laylah Rose, you are the most beautiful young ladies. Grow strong, learn as much as you can, and please live your lives according to your rules only. And, never take wooden nickels! I love you always! Thank you to my mother-in-law and father-in-law, Robert and Donna Fay Hammonds. You two truly are the greatest in-laws anyone could ask for and I know you two were no accident… GOD made this happen. Thank you for everything. I love you! Thank you to my Jack Russell puppy dog, Major. You are the only baby I have been blessed with so far. You changed me. You know when I'm sad, you know when I'm happy. I know we rescued you, but I can't help but to feel as if you rescued me. I love you!

Thank you to my husband, Quentin. You showed up in my life and had to deal with the eye of Category 5, Hurricane Katrina. I was a personal and business storm, but you survived it; we survived it. You understood the vision, we came together to expand it, and we made it better together. Thank you for your unwavering support for this Achiever. I love you!

I love you all!
Truly Yours,
Katrina Mosley Stinnett

Time to Soar!

Like: #COLLECTINGWOODENNICKELS

Join the Discussion in my closed group:
#DRINKSANDCONVERSATIONS

Now is the time to make the decision to stop collecting wooden nickels. It takes courage and faith and some serious soul searching. I shared these stories with you in the hopes of encouraging, inspiring, and empowering you. Take a good look at yourself in the mirror, and if you don't like what you see, it is never too late to change and continue reaching for your dreams.

I definitely want to hear about how you have stopped collecting the wooden nickels in your life.

Please join in the conversation with me in my closed group: Drinks and Conversations, or just leave me a quick comment on the page: Collecting Wooden Nickels.

Website: www.collectingwoodennickels.com

It's time to step out on faith and receive everything life brings!

To connect with Katrina or for bookings, email her at:
collectingwoodennickels@gmail.com
or drinksandconversations@gmail.com

Like the Facebook pages: Collecting Wooden Nickels and Drinks and Conversations

Join the closed discussion group on Facebook: Drinks and Conversations

Website: www.collectingwoodennickels.com

About the Author

Katrina Mosley Stinnett was born in Mobile, Alabama. She is an Army Veteran, empowerment and motivational speaker for community development, and advocate who has worked with the homeless population to provide them with essential needs.

In 2015, Katrina and her husband, Quentin, launched Everything Life Brings, LLC, which serves as the umbrella for several projects including the Alabama Black Expo and Miss Alabama Black Expo Pageant; Queen's Gala; the apparel line, ELB Approved; the home goods line, ELB Essence; and their nonprofit organization, the SOAR ELB Foundation.

Katrina received her associate of science degree from Calhoun Community College, earned her certificate in medical administration from Capps College, and holds an Alabama real estate license. After over two decades of writing, *Collecting Wooden Nickels* is her first published work.

Katrina resides in Huntsville, Alabama. When she is not spending quality time with her family and helping others, Katrina enjoys photography, graphic design, and, of course, writing.

Learn more at
www.collectingwoodennickels.com

CREATING DISTINCTIVE BOOKS
WITH INTENTIONAL RESULTS

We're a collaborative group of creative masterminds with a mission to produce high-quality books to position you for monumental success in the marketplace.

Our professional team of writers, editors, designers, and marketing strategists work closely together to ensure that every detail of your book is a clear representation of the message in your writing.

Want to know more?
Write to us at info@publishyourgift.com
or call (888) 949-6228

Discover great books, exclusive offers, and more at
www.PublishYourGift.com

Connect with us on social media

@publishyourgift

www.ingramcontent.com/pod-product-compliance
Lightning Source LLC
Chambersburg PA
CBHW052054070526
44584CB00017B/2174